LOVE CAME DOWN
Unwrapping the Gift of Our Risen Savior

Janice Wilhelm

Cover design by Janice Wilhelm

Love Came Down: Unwrapping the Gift of Our Risen Savior

Copyright © 2018 by Janice Wilhelm

Published by Wildrose Media

ISBN: 978-1-7327803-0-9 (print book)

ISBN: 978-1-7327803-1-6 (eBook)

CONTENTS

Author's Note	vii
Day 1: Prophecy	1
Day 2: Hope	5
Day 3: Creation and the Need for a Savior	7
Day 4: The Bible, Our Guidebook for Life	11
Day 5: The New Covenant	15
Day 6: The Royal Priesthood	19
Day 7: Purpose	23
Day 8: The Shoot of Jesse	25
Day 9: John the Baptist Prepares the Way	29
Day 10: The Significance of Bethlehem	33
Day 11: Angels as God's Messengers	37
Day 12: Mary - Obedience and Faith	41
Day 13: Joseph - Obedience and Adoption	45
Day 14: Love Came Down - The Birth of Jesus	49
Day 15: Gifts, Part One - Jesus, the Greatest Gift	53
Day 16: The Names of Jesus	55
Day 17: The Significance of the Swaddling Cloths	59
Day 18: Joyful Celebration	63
Day 19: The Shepherds	65
Day 20: The Star	69
Day 21: Gifts Part Two - Treasures from the Magi	73
Day 22: Presentation at the Temple	77
Day 23: Simeon	81
Day 24: Love	85

Contemporary Christmas Songs	89
Acknowledgments	91
About the Author	93
Upcoming Books	95
Notes	97
Notes	99
Notes	101

Dedicated, with love to my mom and dad

AUTHOR'S NOTE

The Christmas season is a special time of food and fun, love and laughter. Reminiscing on Christmases past we eagerly anticipate this year's festivities as we prepare to celebrate with family and friends. Many of us busy ourselves with weeks of preparation - decorating, baking and shopping. As we select gifts for those we love, we remember our greatest gift, the gift of God's Son, Jesus Christ. As Christians, it is important to set aside time to reflect on the awe and wonder of Christ's presence, for it is Jesus who makes this season bright. Only through Him do we have hope and know true love, joy, and peace.

The significance of Christ's birth is found in His purpose. His birth fulfilled God's promise for a Savior, to redeem our sinful hearts. Jesus humbled Himself and lived among us, the almighty, holy God born as a sinless man. His perfect life personified God's holy character, revealing to us pure love and true righteousness. Christ gave us the ultimate gift when He gave up His life, that through His death we might experience life eternal. This is what we celebrate- no longer a helpless babe, Jesus is our risen Lord and Savior.

As we remember the miracle of Christ's birth, we examine the significant details - the prophecies, promises, places, and people which surround this momentous event. Over the next few weeks, through daily reflections, we will unwrap and reveal glimpses of God's divine hand at work in the circumstances which surround His Son's birth.

For many of us, songs are an important part of worship. Listening to and singing Christmas carols are a way of preparing for and celebrating the Advent season. Included with each daily reading are a selection of Christmas carols, traditional hymns, and contemporary songs which tie into that day's theme and focus. You can enjoy familiar songs, or search to discover a new favorite, worshipping God with heart, mind, and voice.

I pray that you will celebrate Christ's birth with wonder and awe as you rejoice in His presence today and hope in His promises for tomorrow.

Have a Blessed Christmas!

Janice Wilhelm

Day 1: Prophecy

This was to fulfill what was spoken through the prophet Isaiah: "Here is my servant whom I have chosen, the one I love, in whom I delight; I will put my Spirit on him, and he will proclaim justice to the nations. He will not quarrel or cry out; no one will hear his voice in the streets. A bruised reed he will not break, and a smoldering wick he will not snuff out, till he has brought justice through to victory. In his name the nations will put their hope."

Matthew 12:17-21, (NIV)

Prophecies are proclamations which foretell or predict future events. Today's reading refers to one of many Old Testament prophecies concerning God's redemptive plan for the world, a plan in place since the beginning of time. These prophecies predict the birth of God's son, Jesus Christ - the Messiah. The title *Messiah* means 'Savior'. God sent Jesus to save mankind from sin and to restore the relationship between man and Creator, which sin had destroyed. The Jewish nation, Israel, were blessed to be God's chosen people and were offered a special relationship with Him. God promised to dwell among them in His Temple and to protect them - as long as they obeyed His laws and kept His commandments.

Many years before Jesus was born, the Israelites strayed

1

from God's will. They chose to live outside of God's laws, and as a result, were punished for their disobedience. The Jews were captured by enemy kings who destroyed God's Temple and brought the Israelites into slavery and bondage. It seemed all hope for their future had been lost. About 600 years before Christ was born, the Jewish people rediscovered the ancient prophecies of a Messiah. The promise of a Savior who would deliver the Israelites from bondage renewed the Jews' hope for their future as a nation.

Sadly, when Jesus Christ came, many Jews rejected Him as their promised Messiah. Jesus arrived as a helpless infant, poor and humble - not at all what the Jews were expecting. Their hope was for an earthly king with a powerful army, who would be able to defeat their enemies. Because of this, the Jewish leaders refused to believe in Jesus and disregarded His teachings. This rejection by His own people was also a fulfillment of prophecy. "He came unto his own, and his own received him not." (John 1:11, KJV) The Jews failed to understand that Jesus provided so much more than the temporary, physical relief they sought. He came not to deliver them from earthly pain and suffering, but to provide forgiveness of sins and eternal life. Through the birth, death, and resurrection of His Son, Jesus Christ, God kept His promise of redemption. God our Father extends this free gift of salvation to all, Jew or Gentile, who place their faith in Jesus Christ as their own Lord and Savior.

Prayer:

Heavenly Father, thank you for sending Your Son, Jesus, as our Savior. We are grateful for Your faithfulness in keeping Your promises. In Jesus' name, Amen.

Songs:

Come Thou Long-Expected Jesus – Charles Wesley, 1744
O Come, O Come, Emmanuel- 9th century, Latin

Day 2: Hope

And again, Isaiah says: The root of Jesse will appear, the One who rises to rule the Gentiles; the Gentiles will hope in Him. Now may the God of hope fill you with all joy and peace as you believe in Him so that you may overflow with hope by the power of the Holy Spirit.

Romans 15:12-13, HCSB

In today's reading, the prophet Isaiah states that God is our source of hope. God offered His Son as a Savior to redeem the fallen world. Jesus was born with this purpose, and His birth fulfilled ancient prophecies. Through His death and resurrection, Jesus offers eternal hope for those who believe in Him. Though we as Christians will still experience pain, frustration, and sorrow, we know that these are temporary afflictions. When Christ returns, we will be given new, immortal bodies that are free from pain, tears, and suffering. This is our hope today.

We live in eager anticipation of Christ's triumphant return, the second Advent. As you reflect on Christ's birth, remember that Jesus is the Hope of all the world. In Christ alone is salvation for those who believe in Him as their Lord and Savior. He loves us and has promised to return for us, so that we may be with Him for all eternity. Come, Lord Jesus, come!

Prayer:

Heavenly Father, our hope is in You alone as we eagerly await Christ's return. Help us be faithful followers and share this hope with others. In Jesus' name, Amen.

Songs:

I Heard the Bells on Christmas Day- H. W. Longfellow, 1863
Our Hope Is Built on Nothing Less– Edward Mote, 1834

Day 3: Creation and the Need for a Savior

*For the word of the L*ORD *is right, and all His work is trustworthy. He loves righteousness and justice; the earth is full of the L*ORD*'s unfailing love...For He spoke, and it came into being; He commanded, and it came into existence...We wait for Yahweh; He is our help and shield. For our hearts rejoice in Him because we trust in His holy name. May Your faithful love rest on us, Yahweh, for we put our hope in You.*

Psalm 33:4-5, 9, 20-22, HCSB

What a powerful God we serve! With mere words, He created the entire universe. We know this to be true as it is documented in God's history book, the Bible. The Bible describes how over a span of six days, the world and its inhabitants came to be. God's spoken command divided the light from darkness and separated water to create dry land. He designed the galaxies as He hung the sun, moon, stars, and planets in their orbits. God spoke and the separation of day and night, the four seasons, and even time itself came into existence. Once the earth was ready, God created vegetation, fish, and animals.

On the sixth day, God took special care when He created a man. God made the man in His image from the dust of the earth. Then He breathed life into this man and gave him a soul. The man's name was *Adam* which means 'man' and 'of the earth'. With the creation of Adam's helpmate, Eve, God created the first family unit and ordained the institution of marriage. Adam and Eve enjoyed a special relationship with God. Together they walked and talked with their Creator in the beautiful garden, called Eden, which He made especially for them. God gave humans the ability to discern right from wrong, and to make decisions and choices affecting their futures. God rested on the seventh day- His creation was complete, and He declared it "very good."

God's original plan for mankind was to be in fellowship with Him and to live in harmony with one another. God gave His most advanced creatures dominion over the earth. Humans were tasked with naming the animals and populating the world with loving caretakers. Sadly, this wasn't enough for Adam and Eve. When they learned they did not possess the knowledge God had, they wished to be wise like Him. Urged by Satan, the deceiver, Adam and Eve disobeyed God by eating fruit from Eden's only forbidden tree, the Tree of Wisdom and Knowledge. With this single act of disobedience, sin entered the entire world. With sin also came the curses of guilt and shame, pain and conflict. Man's work became toil, and creation was in turmoil. Adam and Eve were banned from God's presence and their garden home.

When it seemed as if all hope was lost forever, the Creator lovingly showed grace and mercy to His fallen creation. God Himself enacted the plan He had ready from the beginning of time - a plan to redeem us from our own destructive ways. When the time was right, God sent His son, Jesus, to bear the punishment for our sins. Just as through Adam we all bear sin's curse, so through Christ, all those who believe are cleansed and become acceptable again before God. At Christmas, we remember Jesus' humble birth, and rejoice in His fulfilled purpose on earth = the great gift of salvation.

Prayer:

Father God, thank you for creating this beautiful world we live in. May we be good stewards and thoughtful caretakers of it. We are humbled and awed by the great love and mercy You show us. Thank you for sending Jesus so that we may have a restored relationship with You and hope for our future. In Jesus' name, Amen.

Songs:

Good Christian Men, Rejoice!- tran. 1853, John Mason Neale
All Creatures of Our God and King- St. Francis of Assisi
This is My Father's World – Malthie D. Babcock, pub.1901
God of Wonders- Rebecca St. James, 2002

Day 4: The Bible, Our Guidebook for Life

All Scripture is God-breathed and is useful for teaching, rebuking, correcting, and training in righteousness, so that the servant of God may be thoroughly equipped for every good work.

2 Timothy 3:16-17 (NIV)

The word of God is described by King David as a light unto his path, guiding his way (Psalm 119:105). The Bible is exactly that - our handbook for life, inspired by God, the author of life itself. Though many different translations exist, we as Christians believe that not one word has been altered from God's original intent and purpose. The Bible reveals to us who God is, and His plan and purpose for mankind. The 66 separate books which comprise the Bible are bound together in a common theme, love.

God speaks to us through Scripture, and it is through reading the Bible that we as Christians learn and grow, both in faith and in our relationship with God. Though we will never be able to fully comprehend God, the Bible reveals glimpses of His character. The Bible contains many stories which tell of second chances, forgiveness, and restoration. These stories depict a loving, patient, and forgiving Father who is faithful, just, and in complete control of both heaven and earth. These accounts demonstrate how God can use imperfect people and difficult circumstances to accomplish His will. The Bible also contains guidelines for relationships, finances, worship, and prayer. It cautions against deception by false prophets, dishonest teachers, and of the dangers of worldly living.

The Bible is divided into two main sections, the Old Testament and the New Testament. The Old Testament focuses on the Israelites, God's chosen people. The New Testament begins with Jesus' birth and contains the gospel message. The word *gospel* means 'good news'. These New Testament books contain a record of the greatest story ever told- our salvation through Jesus Christ, God's son. As sinners, we owed a debt to God that we ourselves could never pay. God in His mercy rescued us by offering His Son, Jesus, as our substitute. As the holy and perfect Son of God, Christ alone was able to fully cover the debt of our sin, restoring our relationship with God. Through faith in Jesus Christ, we are adopted as God's children and become heirs of eternal life. The Bible provides us the information necessary to participate in this inheritance. Reading the Bible increases our knowledge of God's will and our purpose, and it also affirms and grows our faith.

Prayer:

Heavenly Father, thank you for giving us Your Word and for Your presence in our lives. We pray You will continue to guide us and give us a deep desire to read Your Word. Allow us to be lights in the darkness of this world and to share Your Word with others so they

may know the true peace, love, and joy that only faith in You can
bring. In Jesus' name, Amen.

Songs:
Light of the World – Mark Chesnutt, 1999
Thy Word – Amy Grant, 1984
I Love to Tell the Story – A. Katherine Hankey, 1866

Day 5: The New Covenant

"The days are coming," declares the LORD, "when I will make a new covenant with the people of Israel and with the people of Judah. It will not be like the covenant I made with their ancestors when I took them by the hand to lead them out of Egypt, because they broke my covenant, though I was a husband to them," declares the LORD. "This is the covenant I will make with the people of Israel after that time," declares the LORD. "I will put my law in their minds and write it on their hearts. I will be their God, and they will be my people".

Jeremiah 31:31-33 (NIV)

Covenant means 'agreement' or 'contract'. A covenant takes place between two or more people who agree on its promises, stipulations, and responsibilities. God Himself established the creation covenant with Adam and Eve. The creation covenant came with certain conditions that God expected them to meet. Compliance with God's mandate- to care for creation, to fill the earth, and to subdue it - would result in abundant blessings for them and their descendants. Disobedience, or the failure to comply with God's will, would result in severe consequences. This was a unilateral covenant - God offered the promises, rewards and punishments and man could offer nothing in return but faith and obedience to Him.

The covenantal relationship between mankind and God was severed when Adam and Eve sinned against God and ate of the forbidden fruit. Despite their disobedience God was not willing to give up on His beloved creation. He enacted a redemptive plan - the covenant of grace. An unconditional covenant, the covenant of grace meant God would rescue mankind from sin, despite man's failures and disobedience. God, in His mercy, promised a Messiah - a Savior, who would crush sin, ensuring that evil would ultimately be overcome. Once redemption occurred, the relationship between God and man could be restored.

God continued to reiterate, and expand upon, these covenantal promises to His chosen people. Inclusion in these covenants was not by personal merit, but by God's own divine will and choice. As a reward for faithful obedience, God promised Abraham that his descendants would be God's own chosen people. Circumcision was a sign of this covenant, and it set the Jews apart from neighboring nations. God later covenanted with Abraham's grandson, Jacob. He changed Jacob's name to Israel, and Jacob became the father of the Israelite nation's twelve tribes, God's chosen people.

When the Israelites were enslaved in Egypt, God sent Moses to lead them to freedom, promising them the land of Canaan as their new home. Following their miraculous escape, God renewed and expanded the Abrahamic covenant between Himself and the Israelites, using Moses as a mediator. At the renewal ceremony, the blood of sacrificed animals was sprinkled first on an altar dedicated to the Lord, and then onto the people of Israel themselves. This blood purified them as a nation and sealed them as God's prized possession. God gave

Moses the 10 commandments and over 600 additional cultural and religious laws for the Israelites to abide by. The Lord promised that if the Israelites kept these laws and obeyed His commandments, He would be their God, and they His people. Blessings would stem from obedience, but disobedience would result in curses upon the entire nation. This covenant was kept by observing the Sabbath and special feast days, obeying strict cleansing rituals, and by offering sacrifices to the Lord. God instituted a new sacrament, the Passover, which would be an annual reminder of God's faithfulness and of the covenantal promises between God and His people.

In today's reading, the prophet Jeremiah foretold the covenant of grace - to be administered by God's own Son, the Messiah. Jesus Christ was born to die. Sacrificed in the place of an unblemished lamb, Jesus' innocent blood covered the debt of all sin completely and eternally. His death fulfilled the requirements of the Mosaic law- complete obedience and sacrifice. The covenant of grace is extended to everyone who believes, both Jews and non-Jews, known as Gentiles. This covenant of grace is personal, between individual believers and God, as opposed to God and the entire nation of Israel. As part of this new covenant, the sacrament of circumcision was replaced with baptism, and Passover with the Lord's Supper, also known as Communion.

There is nothing we can do to earn salvation- it is a gift that God gives freely. Through belief in Christ as our Savior, salvation offers us renewed life. Sin remains in the world for now, but believers are gradually being made righteous through the Holy Spirit working within us. Christians eagerly antici-pate Christ's return when He will establish a new heaven and a new earth. There we will witness the peaceful co-existence of created animals that show hostility towards each other now, and we will experience a relationship with God as He originally ordained it to be.

Prayer:

Heavenly Father, thank you for keeping Your ancient covenantal promises by sending Your son, Jesus. We are grateful for this gift of salvation and look forward to Christ's return when we may experience covenantal life as You desired it to be. In Jesus' name, Amen.

Songs:

Great is Thy Faithfulness – Thomas Chisholm, 1925
Blessed Assurance - Fanny J. Crosby, 1873
In Christ Alone - Stuart Townend, 2001
Blessed Be the God of Israel – Michael Perry, 1973

Day 6: The Royal Priesthood

But you are a chosen people, a royal priesthood, a holy nation, God's special possession, that you may declare the praises of him who called you out of darkness into his wonderful light.

2 Peter 2:9 (NIV)

God had originally intended for the nation of Israel to be a holy nation, a kingdom of priests – a physical representation of what occurs in heaven. Sadly, the Israelites sinfully disobeyed God's laws and rejected God's covenants. God instituted the earthly priesthood to act as mediators between Himself and the Israelites, so that He didn't destroy this nation in His righteous anger. The priests were anointed by God from the tribe of Levi, and it was their duty to represent covenantal living among the Israelites. The Levites led worship, taught the law, and offered ritual sacrifices to God. The Levite high priest held a special place of honor, representing Jesus Christ's position as high priest in heaven. Set apart from the other tribes, the priests wore special garments and lived in designated cities scattered throughout the nation. The priests' entire lives revolved around obedient service to God.

God dwelt among His people in a tabernacle tent during the time the Israelites wandered in the wilderness, and later in the Temple built in Jerusalem by King Solomon. A thick curtain sectioned off the room where the Ark of the Covenant - God's dwelling place - was kept, called the Holy of Holies. Once a year, on the Day of Atonement, the Levite high priest would enter into the Holy of Holies on behalf of the Israelite nation. There he sprinkled the blood of a sacrificed goat on the mercy seat of God. This temporarily satisfied God's requirement that innocent blood be shed for the forgiveness of sins.

Later, during the time of the Judges, a new priesthood was promised – a royal priesthood, one from the royal tribe of Judah. Jesus, as heaven's high priest, would descend and reign on earth. Jesus fulfilled the covenantal moral and ceremonial laws with His shed blood, and perfect obedience to God's will. Following Christ's death, God Himself tore the Temple veil in half from top to bottom, allowing mankind to approach God individually, without needing a priest or mediator. The relationship between God and man was extended to all who believe, both Jew and Gentile.

Now that all believers are members of this royal priesthood, we dedicate our lives as living sacrifices in service to God, as He had originally intended. A new law is now in effect, one that is written on our hearts. The Holy Spirit dwells in us, transforming us to righteousness in our thoughts, words, and deeds. We worship God with our lives when we praise Him, show love and care for others, share the gospel, and live out our God-given purpose in faithful service to our glorious King.

Prayer:

Dear Lord, thank you for sending us Your son, Jesus, as mediator of the new covenant. Thank you for adopting us and granting us the right to be heirs of Your kingdom. In Jesus' name, Amen.

Songs:

Go Tell It on the Mountain – John W. Work, Jr., 1907
Praise My Soul, the King of Heaven- Henry F. Lyte, 1834
We Are A Chosen People, A Royal Priesthood- 1982
Chosen Generation - Chris Tomlin, 2010

Day 7: Purpose

All things are done according to God's plan and decision; and God chose us to be his own people in union with Christ because of his own purpose, based on what he had decided from the very beginning.

Ephesians 1:11 (GNB)

Even before we were born, God had a plan and purpose for each of our lives. Though God's original plan for mankind was tainted by sin, our purpose remains unchanged. We are created to worship God, to be in relationship with Him, and to live according to His will. As image-bearers of Christ in the new covenant, we must conduct ourselves in a manner holy and pleasing to God. We worship Him when our thoughts, deeds, and actions are in alignment with His word. When our lives reflect God's love and righteousness, others will see Christ in us and desire His life-giving grace for themselves.

Each of us has God-given talents and special skills. Using these gifts and developing them to the best of our abilities honors God and is itself an act of worship. Because of sin, our best efforts are often thwarted by factors beyond our control. Despite our frustrations, we can remain hopeful because the

Bible teaches that all things work together to fulfill God's purpose in, and for, our lives.

We are encouraged by the knowledge that though the battle against evil is ongoing, the war has already been won. We have eternal victory in Christ. The birth of Jesus was only the beginning of the redemption story - one that climaxed at Easter and will be complete upon Christ's return, which is the second Advent.

We celebrate Christ's birth with His death and resurrection in mind, for that was Jesus' primary purpose in coming to earth. He fulfilled His purpose, so we could fulfill ours. Hallelujah!

Prayer:

Father God, we ask that You reveal Yourself to us more and more as we read Your Word. Make clear to us what our purpose is and guide us to do Your will. In Jesus' name, Amen.

Songs:

Glorious- For King and Country
I Surrender All – J.W. Van De Venter, 1896
Have Thine Own Way, Lord – Adelaide A. Pollard, 1902
Guide me, O Thou Great Jehovah – William Williams, 1745
Love You with My Life – Bryan Duncan, 2004

Day 8: The Shoot of Jesse

A shoot will come up from the stump of Jesse; from his roots a Branch will bear fruit. The Spirit of the LORD will rest on him— the Spirit of wisdom and of understanding, the Spirit of counsel and of might, the Spirit of the knowledge and fear of the LORD.

Isaiah 11: 1-2 (NIV)

About 600 years before Christ was born, due to their sinful disobedience, God allowed His chosen people to be conquered by the Assyrians and Babylonians. The Jews were scattered, and the Temple destroyed. God allowed the pruning of His people until only small remnant remained. During this time, the royal house of King David lay dormant. Only the words of the prophets, including Isaiah, offered a glimmer of hope for God's remaining people - that there would be a king once again on David's throne. The birth of Jesus, the Messiah, from the tribe of Judah signified new life and renewal - like a new shoot growing from an apparently dead stump.

Jesus, by taking the form of a man, did not empty Himself of His deity. He shed only the magnificent outward manifestation of His glory to become the human image of the invisible God. He was still fully God when He took on the form of a man. Jesus was the perfect example of God's design for

25

humanity, living righteously and without reproach. As a perfect vessel, He was full of life - filled with the Spirit of God. The characteristics of this Spirit illustrate the perfection and divinity of Jesus, and the complete blessing of God.

Filled with the Spirit of wisdom, understanding, and knowledge, Jesus was, and is, able to give perfect counsel. His moral judgement has no bias toward our social status or outward appearance but is based instead on His divine frame of reference.

The Spirit of power is demonstrated in Jesus' authority over nature, sin, life, and death. In humility, Jesus submitted to God the Father. This submission enabled Him to accomplish God's will and purpose on earth, the redemptive plan begun thousands of years before.

The Spirit of the Lord reveals Jesus' ultimate purpose. The long-dormant stump came to life and provides salvation, guidance, and peace to the faithful. He now sits on David's throne and rules eternally. He is the King over all kings and Lord of all Lords.

Prayer:

Heavenly Father, thank you for Your faithfulness, for remembering Your people, and for sending us Jesus. Keep us mindful of the example Jesus gave us through His perfect and blameless life. May we, too, be filled with the Holy Spirit and humbly submit our lives to Your service. In Jesus' name, Amen.

Songs:

Lo. How a Rose E'er Blooming – trans. 1894 by Theodore Baker
Il Est Ne (He is Born)- trad. 19th century French carol
O God Our Help in Ages past- Isaac Watts, 1719
El Shaddai- Michael Card & John Thompson, 1981

Day 9: John the Baptist Prepares the Way

But the angel said to him: "Do not be afraid, Zechariah; your prayer has been heard. Your wife Elizabeth will bear you a son, and you are to call him John. He will be a joy and delight to you, and many will rejoice because of his birth, for he will be great in the sight of the Lord. He is never to take wine or other fermented drink, and he will be filled with the Holy Spirit even before he is born. He will bring back many of the people of Israel to the Lord their God. And he will go on before the Lord, in the spirit and power of Elijah, to turn the hearts of the parents to their children and the disobedient to the wisdom of the righteous - to make ready a people prepared for the Lord."

Luke 1:13-17 (NIV)

John the Baptist came as the final prophet of the old covenant. He was a promised child, the answer to many prayers - a special son sent to fulfill God's purpose. John was filled with the Holy Spirit even before he was born. Set apart from conception, he was to eat no bread and drink no wine. As a man, he lived apart from others in the desert of Judea and wore clothing made of camel skin. John's father, Zechariah, was from the tribe of Aaron, and served as a priest in Jerusalem's temple. God Himself named John, which means

'Jehovah's gracious gift' John was indeed a gift to the Jewish people, preparing their hearts and minds for the coming Messiah. His birth fulfilled a prophecy which promised a messenger to prepare the way for Jesus, "I will send my messenger, who will prepare the way before me" (Malachi 3:1, NIV). The Jews were used to following the Mosaic laws and showing outward signs of obedience to God, but John the Baptist prepared them for a new way of thinking. John taught repentance and the inward reformation of the heart, which leads to transformed lives.

Preaching in Judea, the Jordan Valley, and in the desert areas surrounding Jerusalem, John proclaimed the coming of the Messiah, who would be both the healer of the sick and the forgiver of sinners. John baptized with water for the forgiveness of sins because water signifies cleansing and purification. By introducing the concept of baptism, John prepared the people for the baptism of the Holy Spirit - a spiritual fire which refines and purifies hearts and minds.

John introduced Jesus as the Lamb of God to the Jewish people, declaring their long-awaited Messiah had come. When John baptized Jesus, this act marked the beginning of Jesus' earthly ministry. Jesus would then spend the next three years teaching and preaching to all who would listen about repentance, faith, and kingdom living.

Prayer:

Thank you, Lord, for preparing our hearts for the gift of Your Son, Jesus, as our sacrificial lamb. Please continue to transform our hearts and refine us with the Holy Spirit so we can live our lives holy and pleasing to You. In Jesus' name, Amen.

Songs:

Glorious Things of Thee are Spoken - John Newton, 1779
Beneath the Waters (I Will Rise) - Dallas Frazier, 1967
Come to the Water – Cathy Harris, 1970's

Day 10: The Significance of Bethlehem

"But you, Bethlehem Ephrathah, though you are little among the thousands of Judah, yet out of you shall come forth to Me the One to be Ruler in Israel, whose goings forth are from of old, from everlasting."

Micah 5:2 "NKJV"

Bethlehem is a small town in the hill country of Judea. It is located about six miles southwest of Jerusalem- about a 2.5-hour walk. Also known as the City of David, it is where Israel's King David was born and later anointed as king by the prophet Samuel. It is also where Jacob's beloved wife Rachel was buried after she died during childbirth. Many Jewish prophets had predicted that Jesus Christ, the Messiah, would be born in Bethlehem. How appropriate that Jesus, the king who was to reign eternally on David's throne, would be born in the ancient King David's hometown!

God used the Roman Emperor to call for a census, motivating Joseph and Mary to travel about 80 miles (about 8-10 days' journey) from their home in Nazareth to Joseph's ancestral town of Bethlehem. All citizens of the Roman Empire were required to register and be counted, so they complied. (Today we could travel the same distance in about 2 hours by car). It can be assumed that Mary and Joseph traveled with a group as caravans were the safest way to travel to guard against bandits.

The significance of Christ's birth occurring in Bethlehem is found in nearby *Migdal Eder*, also known as 'The Tower of the Flock'. Migdal Eder is an ancient watchtower described in the Jewish Mishnah (a collection of Jewish oral laws compiled around 200 A.D.) as a place for purified shepherds to watch over a uniquely dedicated flock of sheep. Each ewe's firstborn male was examined carefully. If it was perfect and unblemished, it was designated for sacrifice in Jerusalem's Temple. The blood of these sacrificed lambs symbolized atonement for the sins of the Jewish people, as demanded by God in the law of Moses. The Migdal Eder shepherds had the task of protecting these special lambs and ensuring they arrived safely in Jerusalem. How significant that Jesus, the unblemished, sinless Lamb of God, who would sacrifice His own life for our sins, was born in Bethlehem.

Prayer:

Father God, we marvel at how all things work together to bring about Your will. Thank you for sending Your Son Jesus as our sacrificial lamb, so that through His shed blood, we may partake in Your covenantal promises. In Jesus' precious name, Amen.

Songs:

O Little Town of Bethlehem - Phillips Brooks, 1867
Once in Royal David's City - Cecil Frances Alexander, 1848
Rose of Bethlehem - Steve Green, 1996

Day 11: Angels as God's Messengers

"How can I know this?" Zechariah asked the angel. "For I am an old man, and my wife is well along in years. "The angel answered him, "I am Gabriel, who stands in the presence of God, and I was sent to speak to you and tell you this good news.

Luke 1:18-19, HCSB

Today if you call someone an angel, you probably mean they are thoughtful and kind. The fact is, the word *angel* actually means 'messenger' in both Hebrew (mal'ak) and Greek (aggelos). Angels play important messenger roles throughout the whole Bible, including in the events surrounding Jesus' birth. It was an angel who informed both Zechariah and Mary they would have sons and told them what to name these boys-John and Jesus, respectively. An angel instructed Joseph to remain with Mary and support her miraculous pregnancy. Later, an entire host of angels celebrated over the fields of Bethlehem, alerting the Temple shepherds of the Savior's birth. What a glorious sight that must have been!

The Bible describes angels as immortal beings created by God. They were witnesses to creation, to 'the very foundation of the earth'. Angels are in submission to God and do His bidding. God determined the role of angels to be encouragers, ministers, providers, and protectors of humanity. They communicate God's will to mankind, and assist God in answering prayers, as is recorded in the book of Daniel (Daniel 9:21-22). Though angels have special powers, they are not all-powerful or all-knowing, only God is. It is also important to know that while angels can take on the form of man, they are not glorified humans (and humans do not become angels after death!).

All angels were created holy and initially lived to worship and praise God. But angels also have free will, and the angel Lucifer (also known as Beelzebul or Satan) wanted to be like God. The consequence of his sinful pride was that Lucifer and his followers were banished from heaven. Even now, Lucifer remains in rebellion against God. He is devoted to the deceit and destruction of mankind. Because of sin, we too, are embroiled in a daily spiritual battle - a battle between the forces of good and evil (Ephesians 6:12). Satan and his demons are persistent in their fight to win the hearts and minds of humans before their time on earth runs out.

Our comfort is in knowing that the final outcome of this war has already been decided. Jesus has overcome evil and God has the final victory. Because of Him, we have hope for our future and peace in our hearts. One day, we will be in God's presence, praising and worshipping Him alongside the angels.

Prayer:

Dear Lord, thank you for communicating with us, protecting us and faithfully answering prayer. Please protect us from the evil spirits that loom around us and threaten our hearts and minds. Thank you that we will share in the ultimate victory over darkness through belief in Your risen Son, Jesus. In His holy name, Amen.

Songs:

Hark! The Herald Angels Sing! - Charles Wesley, 1734
Angels from the Realms of Glory - James Montgomery, 1816
King of Angels - Krystal Meyers, 2005
Whom Shall I Fear (God of Angel Armies) - Chris Tomlin, 2012

Day 12: Mary - Obedience and Faith

The angel went to her and said, "Greetings, you who are highly favored! The Lord is with you." Mary was greatly troubled at his words and wondered what kind of greeting this might be. But the angel said to her, "Do not be afraid, Mary; you have found favor with God. You will conceive and give birth to a son, and you are to call him Jesus. He will be great and will be called the Son of the Most High. The Lord God will give him the throne of his father David, and he will reign over Jacob's descendants forever; his kingdom will never end." "How will this be," Mary asked the angel, "since I am a virgin? "The angel answered, "The Holy Spirit will come on you, and the power of the Most High will overshadow you. So, the holy one to be born will be called the Son of God. Even Elizabeth your relative is going to have a child in her old age, and she who was said to be unable to conceive is in her sixth month. For no word from God will ever fail." "I am the Lord's servant," Mary answered. "May your word to me be fulfilled." Then the angel left her.

Luke 1:28-38 (NIV)

Much of what is believed about Mary, the mother of Jesus, is a result of religious tradition, not biblical fact. Some churches teach that Mary is in heaven with God the Father,

Son, and Holy Spirit, where she acts as mediator between us and God. The Bible, however, teaches that Jesus is our mediator, not Mary, and it is only through Christ's atoning sacrifice that we are able to have a personal relationship with God. Some churches teach that Mary is holy and to be revered. Many people believe Mary remained a virgin, did not have more children, and did not experience death. When we examine Scripture however, we see that Mary does not elevate or isolate herself as a special woman in the Jewish community. She marries Joseph and bears him at least four sons and an unknown number of daughters (Matt 13:53-56).

Though a young and ordinary girl, Mary received the great privilege of mothering God's Son, Jesus. Not much is written about her in the Bible, but it is indicated that she was a devout Jewish girl. The angel, Gabriel, calls her 'highly favored' when he greets her. Mary was likely a teenager around 14-16 years old when she became pregnant, a common age for betrothal in those days. Young and unmarried, she displayed God-honoring faith when Gabriel told her of the coming baby. Accepting her role in God's promise, Mary submitted herself in willing obedience, despite what it would cost her personally. Her faith and trust in God's will for her life meant she was able to be mightily used by Him. Through Mary's obedience, God fulfilled prophecy, sending the Messiah - the Jews' promised Savior. Mary believed that nothing was impossible for her God, accepting His immaculate conception with her solid faith.

God demonstrates His power and might by making the impossible possible. We must examine ourselves and ask if we, too, have completely submitted ourselves to Him. When we place our trust and faith in the Lord, He is able to do wondrous works in us, and through us.

Prayer:

Heavenly Father, thank You for showing us that You can use ordinary people to accomplish Your will. Please help us to be obedient and faithful servants like Mary, submitting our lives completely to You. In Jesus' name, Amen.

Songs:

Mary, Did You Know? - Mark Lowry, 1991
Breath of Heaven (Mary's Song) - Chris Eaton
Be Born in Me (Mary) - N. Nordeman & B. Herms, 2011
A Baby Changes Everything - C. Wiseman & T. Nichols, 2004

Day 13: Joseph - Obedience and Adoption

The birth of Jesus Christ came about this way: After His mother Mary had been engaged to Joseph, it was discovered before they came together that she was pregnant by the Holy Spirit. So her husband Joseph, being a righteous man, and not wanting to disgrace her publicly, decided to divorce her secretly. But after he had considered these things, an angel of the Lord suddenly appeared to him in a dream, saying, "Joseph, son of David, don't be afraid to take Mary as your wife, because what has been conceived in her is by the Holy Spirit. She will give birth to a son, and you are to name Him Jesus, because He will save His people from their sins."

Matthew 1:18-21, HCSB

The birth of Jesus required obedient participation and faith from both Mary and Joseph. In ancient Jewish culture, engagements were done in a very specific way. Parents arranged marriages for their children, often without the consent, or even knowledge, of the young bride and groom. Money and gifts, called 'mohar' were given to the bride's family in exchange for their daughter, and a marriage contract was signed by both families. This contract was considered legally binding, even though the actual wedding and consummation would not take place for up to a year afterwards. The termination of a marriage contract could only occur with an official divorce decree from a rabbi.

Imagine Joseph's surprise when Mary, his betrothed, is found to be suddenly pregnant - and he knows he's not the father! Simple logic led Joseph to believe Mary had been unfaithful. Joseph's character was such that he was considering divorcing Mary quietly, so as not to publicly embarrass or disgrace her - even though, according to Jewish law, he could have had her stoned to death for adultery. It was while Joseph was considering what to do that he was visited by the angel Michael in a dream. The angel explained to him that Mary's pregnancy was the fulfillment of Biblical prophecy (Isaiah 7:14). Joseph chose to believe and obey the angel's words and took Mary into his home but did not consummate the marriage until after Jesus was born.

While we recognize Jesus is God's Holy Son, He was also fully human and was raised by an earthly father. Joseph himself was a descendant of King David, from the tribe of Judah, which fulfilled Biblical prophecy concerning Jesus' royal heritage. Joseph adopted Jesus as his own, loved him, and raised him alongside the other children God gave to himself and Mary. The kindness and consideration Joseph demonstrated toward Mary was likely shown to Jesus and his siblings as well. Joseph, as was customary at that time, taught his sons necessary life skills, including his trade - carpentry.

Just as Jesus was adopted by Joseph, we as Christians are given the honor of being adopted by God as His children and are considered co-heirs with Christ of God's eternal blessings. God gave us the Bible and the Holy Spirit to teach us how to live lives pleasing to Him, and how to love others the way God loves us - selflessly and completely.

Prayer:

Heavenly Father, thank You for the example of Joseph's obedience. Grant us the grace and compassion to love others completely as You have loved us and accepted us as Your adopted children. In Jesus' name, Amen.

Songs:

Strange Way to Save the World - Clark/Koch/Harris, 1993
Joseph's Song - Michael Card, 1991
It Wasn't His Child – Skip Ewing, 1990
Take My Life and Let it Be - Frances R. Havergal, 1873

Day 14: Love Came Down - The Birth of Jesus

And it came to pass in those days that a decree went out from Caesar Augustus that all the world should be registered. This census first took place while Quirinius was governing Syria. So all went to be registered, everyone to his own city. Joseph also went up from Galilee, out of the city of Nazareth, into Judea, to the city of David, which is called Bethlehem, because he was of the house and lineage of David, to be registered with Mary, his betrothed wife, who was with child. So it was, that while they were there, the days were completed for her to deliver. And she brought forth her firstborn Son, and wrapped Him in swaddling cloths, and laid Him in a manger, because there was no room for them in the inn.

Luke 2:1-7 "NKJV"

In humility, God's Son entered the world - fully man, yet completely divine. Jesus came to earth as a helpless infant, born to an inexperienced teenage mother - a stranger in an unfamiliar town. His first bed was a feed trough, and his first visitors were lowly shepherds. What great love Christ demonstrated by allowing Himself to live among us, sinful humans! What glory, power, and honor He set aside to fulfill His God-given purpose! He took on the form of a man, so we could know God the Father through Him. Fully human, yet completely righteous, Jesus alone was able to live the perfect, blameless life we had been created to enjoy.

During His time on earth, Jesus demonstrated the holiness of God through His character traits, including love, joy, peace, patience, goodness, gentleness, kindness, humility, and self-control. As a man, Jesus suffered temptation, hunger and thirst, rejection, agony, and death. His sinless responses to these circumstances showed us how we should react to life's often difficult demands.

Today's Scripture reading states that Bethlehem had no rooms in which Mary could give birth. Jesus was rejected, even from the start. He was despised by the leaders and teachers of the law, denied by His own people, the Jews. God knew this would happen, yet still extended the salvation promise to all who believed, both Jew and Gentile. All those who allow God to make room in their hearts, who repent and believe in Christ as their personal Savior, are given the right to become adopted brothers and sisters in Christ - heirs of salvation. At Christmas and always, let us make room in our hearts for our Savior, Jesus Christ.

Prayer:

Dear Lord, we humble our hearts and offer ourselves to Your service. May we demonstrate Christ-like humility so that His sacrificial love for us will be evident in our daily interactions with others. Through our love, cause others to know You and become our brothers and sisters in the faith. In Jesus' name, Amen.

Songs:

Away in A Manger – Anonymous, ca. 1885
Love Has Come- A. Grant, M.W. Smith & J. S. Keister, 1983
Born That We May Have Life– Tomlin/Cash/Maher, 2009
Turn Your Eyes Upon Jesus – Helen H. Lemmel, 1922

Day 15: Gifts, Part One - Jesus, the Greatest Gift

For God so loved the world that He gave His only begotten Son, that whoever believes in Him should not perish but have everlasting life.

John 3:16, "NKJV"

For many of us, the giving and receiving of gifts adds to the excitement of Christmas. Gift giving allows us to show affection and appreciation to others. Selecting the perfect gift takes time and attention. It requires being knowledgeable of the recipient's likes, wants, and needs. The true value of a gift is not in its cost, but in its suitability and purpose.

It is important to remember that the greatest gift of Christmas has nothing to do with shopping malls or credit cards. Nor was it wrapped up in pretty paper with a bow. The gift of God's Son, Jesus, is priceless and precious. By giving us His son, God gave us Himself. Jesus is called *Emmanuel*, which means 'God with us'. God came down to our level so we could know Him, draw near to Him, and communicate with Him in a way that we could understand and comprehend. By freely giving us His son, Jesus, God met our deepest need – that of redemption from sin.

God, our loving Father, continues to meet and exceed all our needs. Through the gift of the Holy Spirit, He provides comfort, conviction, and guidance, as we live out our lives in righteousness and renewal.

Thanks be to God, the giver of eternal life through Jesus Christ - the greatest gift of all!

Prayer:

Loving Father, we come to You again with thankful hearts. You have given us the greatest treasure imaginable in Your son Jesus. Help us to share Your loving gift with others by spreading Your gospel message. In Jesus' blessed name, Amen.

Songs:

Silent Night – Joseph Mohr, 1818
Now Thank We All Our God– M. Rinkart, tr. C. Winkworth
Freely, Freely – Carol Owens, 1972
Jesus, Priceless Treasure- J. Franck, 1653 tr. C. Winkworth, 1863

Day 16: The Names of Jesus

For to us a child is born, to us a son is given; and the government will be upon his shoulder, and his name will be called "Wonderful Counselor, Mighty God, Everlasting Father, Prince of Peace." Of the increase of his government and of peace there will be no end, upon the throne of David, and over his kingdom, to establish it, and to uphold it with justice and with righteousness from this time forth and for evermore. The zeal of the LORD of hosts will do this.

Isaiah 9:6-9, RSV

What is the importance of a name? Our name is a part of who we are, a piece of our identity. It is how others address us to get our attention, and it's what we write on a document to claim it as our own. Parents choose names for their children based on many different factors. For some, it may be to honor a favorite relative, beloved friend, or even an admired book character. For others, a name commemorates a special place or treasured memory. Still other parents decide on a name based on its sound, spelling, meaning, or originality. In Jewish families, parents frequently name their children after relatives, believing the new child would take on admired qualities of their namesake. God Himself chose His Son, Jesus', name to describe His purpose and character.

The angel Gabriel gave Jesus' name to Mary as 'Yeshua'. Yeshua was a fairly common name for Jewish boys at that time. The English equivalent of the Hebrew *Yeshua* is 'Joshua', which remains a popular name today. The New Testament was written in Greek and the Greek version of *Yeshua* is 'Iesous', which when translated into English becomes 'Jesus'. It is important to note that even though the language may change, the nature and meaning of Jesus' name does not. In all languages, the name means 'Savior' or 'Yahweh, the Lord is Salvation'.

The Bible uses about 200 different names for Jesus, not including the 400 additional names which allude to the Holy Trinity of God the Father, Son, and Holy Spirit. Our Scripture passage today lists some attributes of Jesus - descriptive names which reveal the heart of God the Father, define who God the Son is, and tell why He came. We will take a look at each name individually.

· Wonderful Counselor: These two words complement each other. The Hebrew word for wonderful is *pele*, which refers to something 'remarkable', 'uncommon', 'extraordinary', a 'wonder', or a 'miracle'.

A counselor gives advice, but first must get to know his client. Jesus is the perfect counselor because He already knows each of us intimately. He knows our sins, weaknesses, gifts, and talents. Because He also knows our past, present, and future, He knows our needs before we ask. Our Wonderful Counselor is always available to us through prayer.

· Mighty God: The word *God* in Hebrew is *'el,* which means 'strength', and this name refers to Jesus, the Son of God, as a strong and powerful leader. He is the captain of our salvation, and our worthy defender who rescues us from sin and hell's fury.

· <u>Everlasting Father</u>: The Hebrew word *ad* means 'forever', 'of continuing existence', 'eternal', and 'of having no end'. Jesus, while remaining subject to God the Father, is the eternal ruler and head of the church.

· <u>Prince of Peace</u>:

The birth of a Prince is always reason for excitement. The Jews had been promised a powerful leader, a Messiah, who would deliver them from their enemies. As the all-powerful king, Jesus has authority and dominion over creation. The reconciliation Jesus provided through His death and resurrection ushered in a new age – that of the church, and the promise and anticipation of eternal life.

Prayer:

Most Holy God, thank you for revealing Yourself to us through Jesus' names. You are awesome and most worthy of our honor and praise. Give us the courage and desire to spread Your message of love, repentance, and forgiveness, so that at Your name, every knee will bow, and every mouth acknowledge You alone as the Lord of life. In Jesus' precious name, Amen.

Songs:

Emmanuel – Michael W. Smith & Amy Grant, 1989
What A Beautiful Name- B. Ligertwood, Hillsong Worship, 2016
All Hail the Power of Jesus' Name- Edward Perronet, 1779
His Name is Wonderful – Audrey Meier, 1959

Day 17: The Significance of the Swaddling Cloths

In that region there were shepherds living in the fields, keeping watch over their flock by night. Then an angel of the Lord stood before them, and the glory of the Lord shone around them, and they were terrified. But the angel said to them, "Do not be afraid; for see —I am bringing you good news of great joy for all the people: to you is born this day in the city of David a Savior, who is the Messiah, the Lord. This will be a sign for you: you will find a child wrapped in bands of cloth and lying in a manger."

Luke 2: 8-12, NRSV

The group of shepherds to whom the angels appeared were likely Temple shepherds, caring for the flocks of sheep that grazed year-round in the hill country of Bethlehem. Carefully selected lambs from this special herd were destined for sacrifice in Jerusalem's Temple. Sacrifices were made for many reasons, including as cleansing rituals and to offer thanksgiving to God. Once a year at Passover, a perfect and unblemished lamb was sacrificed by the Levite high priest. This sacrifice reminded the Jewish nation of God's protection while they were slaves in Egypt. God had spared their eldest sons' from the angel of death, due to the blood of a lamb placed on their doorposts.

The Temple Shepherds needed to be attentive and observant, especially during lambing season. Only firstborn males - lambs that had 'opened the womb' of an ewe - were eligible for temple sacrifice. When it was discovered that a male lamb had been born, a shepherd would wrap that lamb in strips of cloth to protect the newborn animal from blemish. This swaddled lamb was then placed in a manger for safety. The swaddling cloths were inexpensive strips of fabric also used in lamps and for burning on torches to provide light. Mary and Joseph, unable to find a room to stay in, sought shelter in a cave near Bethlehem, which was used to house animals. These barn-like accommodations meant the cloth strips, used on the Temple lambs, were also readily available to swaddle the newborn baby, Jesus.

It was common practice at this time to rub a newborn in powdered salt and oil, then wrap them tightly in a long strip of cloth. The practice of swaddling was two-fold - first, it would help the child's limbs grow straight, and secondly, it signified the intention of the parents to raise their child to be upright and faithful to God. A swaddling band was lovingly prepared and embroidered by a bride-to-be with symbols and words significant to the couple. It was used during their wedding ceremony to bind the couple's hands together, signifying unity. Following the wedding ceremony, the special cloth was carefully set aside until needed to swaddle the couple's firstborn child. The Bible does not say whether Mary used her special wedding cloth to wrap the newborn Jesus, but the use of a swaddling cloth itself is mentioned twice in the Bible as 'a sign' (Luke 2:12). The fact that Jesus was wrapped in a cloth was not uncommon- what struck the Shepherds as unusual was that He was placed in a manger, just as they did with the temple lambs. It was this detail which confirmed Jesus' identity to the

Shepherds - the promised Messiah, the Lamb of God, had come!

Prayer:

Father God, thank you for wrapping us in Your all-encompassing love. Thank you for shepherding us through life, and for providing Jesus, the unblemished lamb to die in our place. In Jesus' blessed name, Amen.

Songs:

Lamb of God – Twila Paris, 1980's
What Child is This? – William Chatterton Dix, 1865
Noel – Chris Tomlin, 2015

Day 18: Joyful Celebrations

Suddenly a great company of the heavenly host appeared with the angel, praising God and saying, "Glory to God in the highest heaven, and on earth peace to those on whom his favor rests."

Luke 2:13-14 (NIV)

It was just another dark, lonely night for the shepherds on the hills near Bethlehem. Suddenly, an angel appeared, surrounded by brilliant light! The shepherds were terrified by what they saw. Then the angel spoke, and with his words, calmed their fears. The angel brought good news - a cause for celebration, the long-awaited Savior had finally arrived! God's presence, indeed His own holiness, had come to earth, and His glory lit up the night sky.

How appropriate that God used a supernatural being, an angel from heaven, to announce the arrival of His son! The angels' miraculous presence bore testimony to Christ's deity. The angels had been present at creation and were witnesses to man's fall. Now they sang with joy to see redemption draw near. A multitude of the heavenly host joined the messenger angel, and together they praised God. Glorifying God for His faithfulness and love, the angels worshiped their Creator. They were bursting at the seams, filled with joy as they witnessed this momentous occasion. This joyful celebration of the angels was Christ's last moment of glory until after His death and resurrection. The long-promised Messiah had finally come. This Christmas, we celebrate with the angel chorus God's faithfulness and enduring love.

Prayer:

Heavenly Father, we thank You for the gift of Your son, Jesus. You shone your great love and light into this dark world. May we ever praise and worship You! In Jesus' name, Amen.

Songs:

The First Noel- traditional English carol
Joy to the World – Isaac Watts, 1719
Joyful, Joyful We Adore Thee- Henry van Dyke, 1907

Day 19: The Shepherds

When the angels had left them and gone into heaven, the shepherds said to one another, "Let us go now to Bethlehem and see this thing that has taken place, which the Lord has made known to us." So they went with haste and found Mary and Joseph, and the child lying in the manger. When they saw this, they made known what had been told them about this child; and all who heard it were amazed at what the shepherds told them.

Luke 2: 15-18, NRSV

Shepherds took shifts watching over the flocks - both day and night, ready to assist any animal in need and protect the sheep from harm. They stayed awake while the rest of the town slept, and therefore, it was the shepherds to whom the angel appeared to announce Jesus' birth.

Shepherding was considered a lowly job in the Jewish community. Jewish law designated anyone who touched dead animals or their excrement as ceremonially unclean. As a part of their daily routine, shepherds were exposed to animal feces while walking in the fields. At times, they were required to touch dead sheep and lambs. According to religious law, these tasks kept the shepherds in a perpetual state of impurity. This meant they were not permitted to offer sacrifices or be in the presence of God at the Temple. Unable to join in communal worship and isolated from society, the shepherds developed personal relationships with Jehovah God.

In contrast, the religious leaders of the Jews kept all the rules, doing exactly as God had demanded in the law of Moses. Believing they could earn God's favor by their actions; these men were very proud of their strict obedience. To remain ritually pure, these leaders avoided contact with anyone whom they considered unclean or impure. Though they strictly kept the Mosaic laws, they were missing a personal relationship with God. Their knowledge of God was head-knowledge, not heart-knowledge.

It is surely significant that God chose these outcast, lowly shepherds over powerful religious leaders to be the first to greet and worship His son! Through this sign, we are once again reminded that Jesus came for ALL people, not just the educated, wealthy, or pious. Christ's birth ushered in a new era - with Jesus as our mediator before God, we are all welcome to a personal relationship with Him. God does not want rule followers; He wants believer's hearts.

Prayer:

Heavenly Father, thank you for enabling us to know You personally, and to communicate with You in prayer. May we share Your love with others, so they too will come to know You and experience Your saving grace. In Jesus' name, Amen.

Songs:

The Little Drummer Boy – Katherine Kennicott Davis, 1941
The First Noel – traditional English carol
While Shepherds Watched their Flocks by Night– N. Tate, 1700
Savior, like a Shepherd Lead Us– D. A. Thrupp, 1836
If We're Honest – Francesca Battistelli, 2014

Day 20: The Star

After Jesus was born in Bethlehem in Judea, during the time of King Herod, Magi from the east came to Jerusalem and asked, "Where is the one who has been born king of the Jews? We saw his star when it rose and have come to worship him."

Matthew 2:1-2 (NIV)

One of the great mysteries of Christ's birth is the origin of the special star, known as the 'star of Bethlehem.' Its appearance was significant enough to prompt Magi to embark on a long and likely dangerous journey to pay homage to a new king. The Magi were a priestly caste of learned men and ancient astronomers, generally believed to have resided in ancient Babylonia, Persia, or Arabia. Scholars and scientists have studied celestial events occurring around this time and have developed theories about this special light. Some theories, such as the possibility of comets and supernovas, have, for the most part, been discredited, but investigations into the star's origin continue.

Central to the investigation is the date of Herod's death. Most scholars agree Herod died in 4 B.C., though new evidence of a data translation error may place his death 3 years later, in 1 B.C. Herod ordered the death of all males in Judea under age two while trying to annihilate the infant Jesus. It was also Herod who met with the Magi when they came to Jerusalem seeking the new king. For these reasons, Herod had to have been alive at the time Christ was born.

Therefore, determining Herod's date of death can provide significant external proof for these Biblical events.

Examination of the night sky between 3 B.C. and 2 B.C. using computer generated re-enactment discloses interesting celestial events. On September 11, 3 B.C., at the beginning of the Jewish New Year (Rosh Hashanah), the sun rose in the constellation of Virgo, which means 'the Virgin'. Around this time, in the constellation of Leo, Jupiter, also called the 'Ruler' planet came into conjunction with (appeared very close to) the 'King' star, Regulus. Jupiter passed close to Regulus twice more within a span of three months in 2 B.C.- on February 17 and May 8. On June 17, Jupiter passed close to Venus, and for about one hour, the proximity of these two bright planets created a brilliant light which would have been visible to the naked eye. Jupiter began retrograde movement (the appearance of moving in the direction opposite other celestial bodies) during the Hanukkah season of gift giving. This retrograde motion made it appear that Jupiter was at a standstill in the sky for a period of six days, one of which was December 25, 2 B.C. Viewed from Jerusalem, and looking towards Bethlehem, it would seem Jupiter had stopped over the little town.

The symbolism and imagery in these events is powerful and poignant. Leo, the lion, is the symbol for the tribe of Judah, from which the Messiah was to come. Both the "Ruler" planet, Jupiter, and the "King star," Regulus, point to the prophecy that Jesus would be a King, as indeed He was. The sun travelling through Virgo in early September may symbolize the newly-pregnant Mary. Finally, Rosh Hashanah -

the Jewish New Year, indicates new beginnings, just as God was beginning the new covenant with His people.

The Bible affirms "the heavens declare the glory of God" (*Psalm 19:1 NIV*). God chose a brilliant, celestial light to signify Christ's presence as a physical manifestation of His glory on earth, as He did on several other occasions in the Bible. He appeared as a burning bush to Moses, a pillar of fire leading the Israelites at night, and the blinding light to Christian persecutor Saul before his conversion to the evangelist Paul.

As compelling as these theories are, some unanswered questions remain. It could be that this light was of purely supernatural design, incomprehensible to our human minds - a special sign created solely for Christ's incarnation. God, the Creator of the universe, is not bound by the laws of nature and can alter them at will. Whatever its cause, the star served its purpose by announcing the birth of Christ and prompting the Magi to travel. Jesus Himself declared, "I am the Light of the world." Jesus' birth marks the beginning of a new era, a dividing line where sin's evil darkness is overcome by Christ's holy light.

Prayer:

Heavenly Father, as we consider the works of Your hands and the universe You created, we stand in awe of You. Everything in heaven and earth is under Your command, created to suit Your purpose. Thank you for sending Jesus, so we may no longer walk in the darkness of sin, but in the light of eternal life. In Jesus' name, Amen.

Songs:

O Holy Night – J.S. Dwight & A.C. Adam, 1847
Brightest and Best – Reginald Heber, 1811
Do You Hear What I Hear? – Noel Regney, 1962
Battle Hymn of the Republic – Julia Ward Howe, 1861

Day 21: The Gifts Part Two - Treasures from the Magi

After hearing the king, they went on their way. And there it was - the star they had seen at its rising. It led them until it came and stopped above the place where the child was. When they saw the star, they were overwhelmed with joy. Entering the house, they saw the child with Mary his mother, and falling to their knees, they worshiped him. Then they opened their treasures and presented him with gifts: gold, frankincense, and myrrh.

Matthew 2:9-11, HCSB

God used celestial bodies to announce the arrival of His son, Jesus. The rising of a special star was noted by Magi, believed by some to be Zoroastrian priests from Persia. To these foreign astronomers, the star was a sign of a new king in Judea. Desiring to honor this new king, the Magi embarked on a journey westward, bearing valuable gifts. At this time in history it was common for foreign nations to honor new rulers with expensive gifts as a sign of homage, peace and goodwill.

While most modern-day depictions of these 'wisemen' portray three men of various ages and ethnicity, that description is based on tradition rather than true Biblical fact. Scripture allows only that there were more than one, and that they presented at least three gifts to Jesus.

The costly gifts of gold, frankincense, and myrrh are them-selves symbolically significant in the account of Christ's birth. Gold, a pure and precious metal, was a symbol of Christ's divinity, kingship, and glory. The glory of God is often depicted as a bright, shining light, like the gold kings used to adorn their palaces and to flaunt their wealth. Frankincense was used in religious rituals and ceremonies. It is an incense which gives off a sweet-smelling smoke when burned. Frankincense signifies purity and prayer and represents God's holiness and righteousness. Myrrh was very difficult to obtain, which made it even more valuable than gold. Known to have medicinal properties, it was used to ease pain. The bitter sap was mixed with wine vinegar and offered to Christ to ease his pain while He hung on the cross. Myrrh was also commonly used as an embalming ointment to prepare bodies after death. A symbol of Christ's mortality, it foreshadowed His death on the cross.

Together these gifts honor Christ as our prophet, priest, and king. The homage by the foreign Magi foretold the extension of God's covenant to all people – including not just the Jews, but the Gentiles as well.

Prayer:

Heavenly Father, to You alone be all glory, praise, and honor. Thank you for sending Your Son as our prophet, priest, and king. May we live our lives in constant gratitude for Your wonderful gift. In Jesus' name, Amen.

Songs:

We Three Kings- John H. Hopkins, Jr., 1857

O Come All Ye Faithful – John Francis Wade, ca. 1743

Jesus Shall Reign – Isaac Watts, 1719

Day 22: Presentation at the Temple

When the time came for the purification rites required by the Law of Moses, Joseph and Mary took him to Jerusalem to present him to the Lord (as it is written in the Law of the Lord, "Every firstborn male is to be consecrated to the Lord"), and to offer a sacrifice in keeping with what is said in the Law of the Lord: "a pair of doves or two young pigeons."

Luke 2:22-24 (NIV)

Remember that Jesus was born into a devout Jewish family and culture. Scripture tells us that Jesus had been circumcised according to the sign of the covenant between God and His people since the days of Abraham. Mary and Joseph were careful to follow the requirements of Mosaic law. Their obedience to these laws secured Jesus' place as a full-fledged member of Jewish society. This fulfilled the prophecy that the Messiah would be born 'under the law.' The priests and Jewish leaders could not deny Jesus' heritage or religious affiliation. Christ's future rejection by His own people was a result of what He taught, not because of who He was as a Jewish man.

Shortly after his birth, Mary and Joseph took Jesus to Jerusalem to complete their lawful duties. These obligations included Mary's purification and the Presentation of the Firstborn Male. Jewish women are considered holy vessels used by God for the creation of human life. Childbirth is also a holy act, as Jews believe God Himself is present, breathing life into the child as it is born. After giving birth, Jewish women enter a state of ritual impurity, as life has left her body. The length of a woman's impurity is dependent upon the newborn's gender- 7 days for a male, 14 days for a female. The time span is longer following the birth of a daughter, as daughters are future bearers of life themselves.

After the initial 1-2 weeks has passed, the woman enters a second phase of ceremonial impurity. This second time period lasts either 33 days after the birth of a son or 66 days after a daughter's birth. To mark the end of their impurity, Judean women are required to offer two sacrifices. These offerings - a burnt offering and a sin offering, allow the woman to be considered ceremonially clean, and to once again fully partici-pate in Jewish society. Jesus' mother, Mary, provided two birds for the temple priest to sacrifice on her behalf. One bird was sacrificed as a sin offering, and the other as the burnt offering. Birds were an acceptable substitute for the preferred unblem-ished lamb provided by those who could afford it.

Once again considered ritually pure, Mary was allowed into the Temple court. She went with Joseph to present Jesus to God. Per Mosaic law, firstborn males, both human and animal, belong to the Lord. Upon presenting their firstborn son to the priests, Jewish parents had a choice to make. They could pay the priests a fee of five shekels to redeem their son from this obligation, or they could consecrate their son's life to the service of God. No redemption price is mentioned at the presentation of Jesus. Jesus had been born to serve God's purpose as the Messiah for His people. His entire life, His very presence on earth, was to accomplish a task only He could accomplish. Though all Jewish families were obligated to perform this ritual, it was significant that Jesus was presented by Mary and Joseph. It implies they accepted that their son - God's Son - had a higher purpose beyond their comprehension.

———— ୦୦♡୦୦ ————

Prayer:

Heavenly Father, thank you for the example of godly parents You gave through Mary and Joseph's obedience. May we also seek Your will and purpose in our lives and offer ourselves fully to Your service. In Jesus' name, Amen.

Songs:

Who is He in Yonder Stall – Benjamin R. Hanby, 1866
Blessed be the God of Israel – Michael Perry, 1973
Hail to the Lords Anointed – James Montgomery, 1821
Jesus is All the World to Me – Will L. Thompson, 1904

Day 23: Simeon

Now there was a man in Jerusalem called Simeon, who was right-eous and devout. He was waiting for the consolation of Israel, and the Holy Spirit was on him. It had been revealed to him by the Holy Spirit that he would not die before he had seen the Lord's Messiah. Moved by the Spirit, he went into the temple courts. When the parents brought in the child, Jesus, to do for him what the custom of the Law required, Simeon took him in his arms and praised God, saying: "Sovereign Lord, as you have promised, you may now dismiss your servant in peace. For my eyes have seen your salvation, which you have prepared in the sight of all nations: a light for reve-lation to the Gentiles, and the glory of your people Israel. "The child's father and mother marveled at what was said about him.

Luke 2:25-33 (NIV)

When Joseph and Mary traveled to Jerusalem to complete the birth rituals required by Mosaic law, they did not know that God had arranged a divine appointment for them. Waiting within the Temple courts was a man named Simeon, one of God's devoted servants. Simeon had been promised by the Holy Spirit that he would not die before witnessing the Messiah with his own eyes. Now that promise was about to be fulfilled as another example of God's loving faithfulness to those who are obedient to Him.

In the Old Testament, the Holy Spirit was only gifted to a few people, for a specific task or purpose. This privilege was given to men who were faithful and willing to be used for God's divine purposes. Simeon was one of these chosen few. He had been selected for a special role - to be a witness to the Messiah's birth.

Old Testament Law required two or three witnesses to confirm an event as truth. The angels and shepherds were the first witnesses to Christ's birth, Simeon the second. Prompted by the Holy Spirit, Simeon entered the temple courts the day of Jesus' Presentation. In heeding the Lord's voice, Simeon was greatly rewarded. His face lit up with joy as he reached for the tiny child, recognizing Jesus as the long-awaited redeemer. As he took God's precious gift in his hands, he proclaimed Jesus as Messiah - the promised One who had come to save both Jew and Gentile. Simeon's waiting was over. His purpose had been fulfilled. Simeon was at peace, He had witnessed God's promised salvation.

As Christians, we are also called to be witnesses for Christ. We are to share the good news of salvation and the promise of eternal life to all who will listen. The Holy Spirit dwells within all believers, to embolden and enable us to do God's will. As we faithfully serve the Lord, we wait with eager expectation for Christ's second Advent. Like Simeon, our anticipation builds as we wait for the day of indescribable joy when Christ will return, and we can live with Him in everlasting peace.

Prayer:

Dear Lord, please help us be obedient to Your will. Let us heed Your voice and allow You to use us according to Your purpose. May we be dutiful witnesses to others of Your love and faithfulness. In Jesus' name, Amen.

Songs:

Good Christian Men Rejoice – trans. John Mason Neale, 1800's
It is Well with My Soul – Horatio G. Spafford, 1873
Have Thine Own Way, Lord – Adelaide A. Pollard, 1902
O Jesus, I Have Promised – John D. Bode ca. 1866

Day 24: Love

Dear friends, let us love one another, for love comes from God. Everyone who loves has been born of God and knows God. Whoever does not love does not know God, because God is love. This is how God showed his love among us: He sent his one and only Son into the world that we might live through him. This is love: not that we loved God, but that he loved us and sent his Son as an atoning sacrifice for our sins. Dear friends, since God so loved us, we also ought to love one another. No one has ever seen God; but if we love one another, God lives in us and his love is made complete in us.

John 4:7-12 (NIV)

Love is not a feeling, it is an action word. As humans, demonstrating love for one another takes time, effort and often great patience. In contrast, God's love is pure and everlasting. In His faithfulness God did not give up on us despite our sinful disobedience. Instead, demonstrating great love and mercy God provided a means of reconciliation, redemption and restoration. He lovingly sent His Son, Jesus to pay the price of our sin. Jesus is the physical evidence of God's love come down to live among us.

When Jesus ascended to heaven, He did not leave us abandoned, but sent His Holy Spirit to dwell within believers. The

Holy Spirit actively teaches, comforts, admonishes, and emboldens us to share the gospel and empowers us to demonstrate Christ's self-sacrificing love to others.

Only through the Holy Spirit working in us are we are able to fulfill Gods great commands - first, to love the Lord God above all else, and second, to love our neighbor as our self. Through the inner working of the Holy Spirit in our hearts, we are transformed into new creatures, righteous and sanctified. The fruits of the Spirit - love, joy, peace, patience, goodness, faithfulness, kindness, gentleness and self-control - are revealed in our lives by what we think, do, and say. We must commit daily to be outward examples of Christ's Spirit here on earth.

May this Christmas be blessed with the richness of God's love, remaining mindful of His faithfulness to us from generation to generation. May we seek to do His will and look forward to glory when we will be greeted with God's words, "Well done, my good and faithful servants!" Oh, what a day that will be! Come, Lord Jesus, come!

Prayer:

Heavenly Father, thank you for Your abiding, abundant, and redeeming love. We pray that our lives might reflect Your love to others and glorify You in all that we do. In Jesus' name, Amen.

Songs:

We Are the Reason- David Meece, 1993
What Wondrous Love is This – USA Folk hymn, 1811
Oh, the Deep, Deep Love of Jesus – Samuel T. Francis, 1875
Pass It On – Kurt Kaiser, 1969

More Contemporary Christmas Songs

A Cradle Prayer by Rebecca St. James

Advent Hymn by Christy Nockels

A Prayer For Every Year by Plus One

A Strange Way to Save the World by Rob Blaney

All is Well by Michael W. Smith

All My Heart Rejoices by Steve Green

Away In a Manger by Brandon Heath

Be It Unto Me by Craig & Dean Phillips

Celebrate the Child by Michael Card

Child of Bethlehem by Wayne Watson

Child of Peace by Sandi Patty

Christmas Day by Michael W. Smith

Christmas is Here by JJ Heller

Christmas is in the Heart by Steven Curtis Chapman

Christmas to Remember by Amy Grant

Gloria by Michael W. Smith

Glorious by for KING & COUNTRY

Going Home for Christmas by Steven Curtis Chapman

Good News by Kathy Mattea

Hallelujah (Light Has Come) by Barlow Girl

Happy Birthday, Jesus by the Brooklyn Tabernacle Choir

How Many Kings by Downhere

I Celebrate the Day by Relient K

Immanuel by Michael Card

It's the Thought by Twila Paris

Jesus is Born by Steve Green

Joy (To the World) by Avalon

Labor of Love by Andrew Peterson

Light of the World by Lauren Daigle.

Little Town by Amy Grant, Point of Grace

No Eye Had Seen by Michael W. Smith, Amy Grant

Not That Far From Bethlehem by Point of Grace

One King by Point of Grace

One Small Child by David Meece

Precious Promise by Steven Curtis Chapman

Real by Nichole Nordeman

Rose of Bethlehem by Steve Green

Sing Mary Sing by Jennifer Knapp

Somewhere In Your Silent Night by Casting Crowns

Still Her Little Child by Ray Boltz

Sweet Little Jesus Boy by Rebecca St. James

Tennessee Christmas by Point of Grace

The Christmas Hope by NewSong

The Christmas Shoes by NewSong

The Heart of Christmas by Matthew West

The Last Christmas Without You by Sixpence None the Richer

The Night That Christ Was Born by Kirk Franklin

This Baby by Steven Curtis Chapman

This Gift by Point of Grace

This Little Child by Scott Wesley Brown

To the Mystery by Michael Card

Unto Us (Isaiah 9) by Sandi Patty

Where's the Line to See Jesus? by Becky Kelley

Winter Snow by Chris Tomlin and Audrey Assad

ACKNOWLEDGMENTS

This book could not have been written without the support and advice from family, friends and writing professionals. First, I would like to thank God for placing this project on my heart and for His unfailing love and faithfulness.

I'd like to offer heartfelt thanks to my book editor, Lib Noori and my cover editor, Kate Padilla for sharing their expertise and guidance. A huge "thank you" to my extremely talented formatter, Jill Michaels for her creative ideas and immense patience with my indecision!

Many friends, family members and acquaintances offered me encouragement, support, advice, and suggestions during my writing process. I would like to acknowledge a few who were especially helpful. I would like to thank Gail Baity for her cheerful spirit of encouragement and sound Biblical advice. To Mindy Kammer for our poolside chats, and for offering of her precious time, her heartfelt encouragement and helpful suggestions. To Debi Huntt Nicholson for her prayers and for reaching out with phone calls when I had become a self-imposed hermit.

Thank you to my dear cousin, Bernice Reimer for her kind and encouraging words, her prayers and offers of assistance from afar. To Theresa, Susan, Margaret, and Mindy for graciously offering of their time to read and critique my draft. To my mom, Margriet Talen for providing me loving guidance, helpful suggestions, a listening ear and unwavering support throughout this entire journey. Last, but certainly not least, to my family - my husband John and my kids, Derek and Jocelyn - thank you for believing in my ability to complete this project, for cheering me on, and for never tiring of hearing my revisions. I will be forever grateful for your patience, love and understanding. I love you.

Janice Wilhem: janicewilhelmauthor@gmail.com
Lib Noori: libhnoori@gmail.com
Kate Padilla: www.blondiemarie.com
Jill Michaels: bestbookformatter.com

ABOUT THE AUTHOR

A bookworm and avid researcher, Janice Wilhelm enjoys discovering the 'behind the scenes' details which make history interesting. Born and raised in Canada, Janice resides in Maryland, USA with her husband and their two children.

UPCOMING BOOKS

Friendship and Freedom: The Statue of Liberty
Owney, the Postal Dog
Our Neighbors to the North

Teaching Series:
Bible Basics for Kids – and their Parents!

Notes

Notes

Notes